The Lullaby Treasury

Mathilde Polee and Petra Rosenberg

The Lullaby Treasury

Cradle Songs from around the World

Floris Books

Unless otherwise noted songs are translated by Polly Lawson

Illustrations by Veronica Nahmias

First published in Dutch under the title *Als je gaat slapen zal ik zingen*
by Christofoor Publishers in 1997
First published in English in 1997 by Floris Books

Acknowledgements:
By the embers' dying glow (p.7), from *Fahr mein Schifflein, fahre,* Edition Bingenheim/Freies
Geistesleben.
The evening wind softly blows (p.12), from *Pirzel und Purzel,* Bärenreiter, Kassel.
Ahrirang (p.21), from *Just Five,* International Music Publishers.
Daylight has passed away (p.31) from *Alles wordt nieuw,* Uitgeverij G.F. Callenbach, Baarn.
Nina bobo (p.42), Wieteke van Dort, the Hague.
O Lord, abide with us (p.55), Bärenreiter, Kassel.
The sandmen (p.62), and The beech tree (p.63), from *Schwinge, schwengel, schwinge,* De Zevenster, Zeist.

British Library CIP Data available

ISBN 0-86315-258-9

Printed in Belgium

Foreword

In every country and culture, lullabies and cradle songs are sung or chanted to help babies and young children go to sleep peacefully. The lullaby, whatever its origin, instinctively takes a recognizable form. The gentle melody provides its own calming magic. The quietly repetitive pattern of the words fills the child's sleepy awareness with a restful, comforting and familiar message: all is safe, all is well.

In practical terms, it is the loving attention flowing to the child that matters, regardless of whether the parent or adult can sing very well or not. As time goes on, the child will want to join in a familiar song, so it is important not to pitch the singing too low. Experience shows, too, that it is a good idea to keep a particular lullaby or two for difficult occasions, such as times of sorrow or illness. This song will then come to acquire a special character as a help.

We hope that this collection of lullabies – chosen from countries and cultures all over the world – will find their way into many homes and places where children are cared for with love, and above all into many children's hearts.

Mathilde Polee and Petra Rosenberg

By the embers' dying glow

Heiner & Marianne Garff, Germany

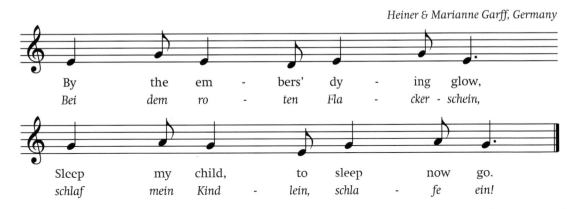

By the em - bers' dy - ing glow,
Bei dem ro - ten Fla - cker - schein,

Sleep my child, to sleep now go.
schlaf mein Kind - lein, schla - fe ein!

2 Now the last flame flickers low,
 Sleep my child, to sleep now go.

3 Hearth-warmth to your eyelids flow,
 Sleep my child, to sleep now go.

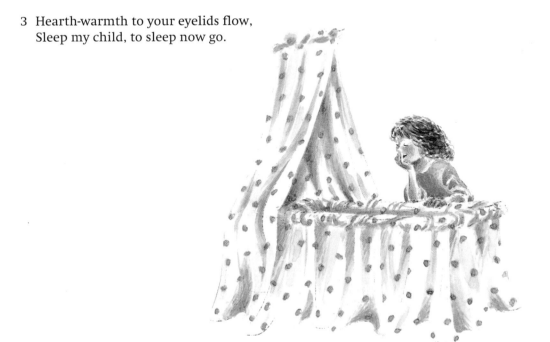

The moon is risen

Der Mond ist aufgegangen

Matthias Claudius   *Johann Abraham Schultz, Germany*

Oh see the moon is ri - sen and gol-den stars are shi - ning in
Der Mond ist auf - ge - gan - gen, die gold-nen Stern-lein pran - gen am

deep dark clear-est sky. The woods are still and fro - zen, the
Him - mel hell und klar. Der Wald steht schwarz und schwei - get und

wind no long-er whi - ning while wisps of mist are float-ing by.
aus der Wie - se stei - get der wei - ße Ne - bel wun - der - bar.

2 How silent is the world now
   Wrapp'd in the cloak of dark night
   And peace is wide and deep.
   Her magic sheen unfurléd
   The moon sends down her soft light
   To charm our sweetest dreaming sleep.

3 Then all the woes of daytime
   And all besetting trouble
   Sink softly into nought.
   Then come the elves to frolic
   And happiness to share out,
   And find what they have always sought.

Sleep, come quick

Traditional from Auvergne, France

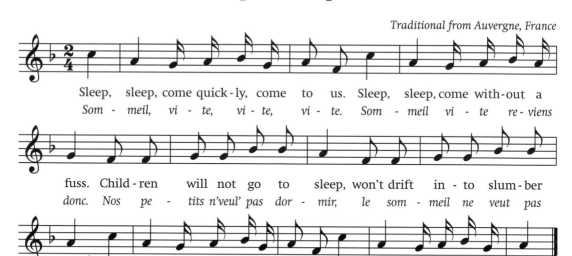

Sleep, sleep, come quick-ly, come to us. Sleep, sleep, come with-out a
Som - meil, vi - te, vi - te, vi - te. Som - meil vi - te re - viens

fuss. Child-ren will not go to sleep, won't drift in-to slum-ber
donc. Nos pe - tits n'veul' pas dor - mir, le som - meil ne veut pas

deep. Sleep, sleep, come quick-ly and send our ba - bies off to deep-est sleep.
v'nir. Som - meil, vi - te, vi -te, vi - te. Som - meil en -dors nos pou - pons.

2 Sleep, sleep, come along quick, quick, quick.
Sleep, sleep, come along quick.
For the boy, wide open eyes
And the girl looks at the skies.
    Sleep, sleep...

Sinhalese lullaby

Traditional Sri Lanka

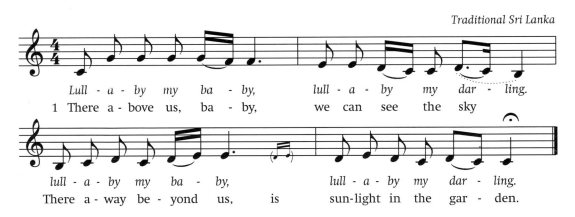

Lull - a - by my ba - by, lull - a - by my dar - ling.
1 There a - bove us, ba - by, we can see the sky

lull - a - by my ba - by, lull - a - by my dar - ling.
There a - way be - yond us, is sun - light in the gar - den.

    Lullaby my baby ...
2 Where, my little one, has your mother gone?
  She goes to the pond where the blue lilies grow

    Lullaby my baby ...
3 When at night, my son, clouds come o'er the moon,
  Then it's time, my son, to sleep and cease to cry.

The evening wind softly blows

Pirzel und Purzel

Ingeborg Klose   Waltraud Klein, Switzerland

Ev' - ning wind now soft - ly blows o'er the wea - ry moun - tain,
Lei - se geht der A - bend - wind durch die mü - den Ber - ge,

lit - tle birds to rest they go, soft - ly sings the foun - tain.
schläf - rig auch die Vög - lein sind und die klei - nen Zwer - ge.

Black eyes

Czech

Lit - tle black eyes, go to sleep. Lit - tle black eyes lie down and
Čer - né o - či, jdě - te spát, čer - né o - či jdě - te spát,

sleep till morn-ing sun will peep, till morn-ing sun will peep.
však mu - sí - te rá - no vstát, však mu - sí - te rá - no vstát.

2 Come the morning, come the day,
   Little black eyes rise, go to play.
   But you must go to sleep
   Till morning sun will peep.

The Christ-Child's lullaby

Taladh Chriostä

Traditional Scottish Highland

My joy, my love, my dar - ling child! My trea - sure
Mo ghaol, mo gradh, is m'eud - ail thu! Gur m'iunn - tas

new, my rap - ture you! My come - ly beau - teous ba - by
ùr is m'eibh - neas thu! Mo mhac - an àl - ainn, ceut - ach

son, un - wor - thy I to tend such one. Hal - le -
thu! cha'n fhiu mi fhein a bhi ad dhàil.

lu - i - a Hal - le - lu - i - a

Hal - le - lu - i - a Hal - le - lu - i - a.

2 Bright son of hope and light you are!
   Of love your heart and eye are made.
   Tho' but a tender babe, I bow
   In heav'nly rapture down to you.
      Halleluia, halleluia, halleluia, halleluia

Close your eyes
Ferme tes yeux

Traditional Breton from France

Close your sweet eyes my dear, Your mo-ther is rock-ing your
Fer - me tes yeux, tout doux! Ta mère est i - ci, mon

cra - dle here. Oh hush-a-by now, oh hush-a-by now, my
bel en - fant, à te veil -ler, à te her - cer, pe-

dear, my dear. Your mo-ther is here, so do not have
tit ché - ri. Ta mère est i - ci, ton père est là

fear, Though fa-ther's a - way Till break of the day, He will see you here.
haut, tan tan di - ra tan tan tan di - ra tan tan tan di - ra do!

My little child

Traditional German from Moravia

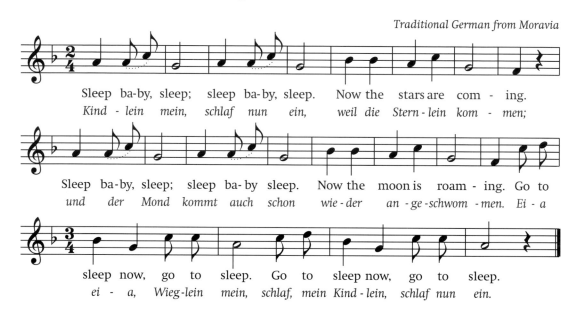

Sleep ba-by, sleep; sleep ba-by, sleep. Now the stars are com - ing.
Kind - lein mein, schlaf nun ein, weil die Stern - lein kom - men;

Sleep ba-by, sleep; sleep ba-by sleep. Now the moon is roam - ing. Go to
und der Mond kommt auch schon wie - der an - ge -schwom - men. Ei - a

sleep now, go to sleep. Go to sleep now, go to sleep.
ei - a, Wieg-lein mein, schlaf, mein Kind - lein, schlaf nun ein.

Do, do, l'enfant do

Traditional French

Doh doh, dar - ling doh. Dar - ling soon to sleep shall go
Do, do, l'en - fant do, l'en - fant dor - mi - ra bien vi - te.

Doh doh, dar - ling doh. Dar - ling soon to sleep shall go.
Do, do, l'en - fant do, l'en - fant dor - mi - ra bien - tôt.

Evening song

Alois Künstler, Germany

O an - gel mine, pro - tect me fine, night and day,

ear - ly and late. Un - til my soul en - ters hea - ven's gate.

Mm mm. O an - gel mine, pro - tect me fine.

Hush, my dear

Traditional Scottish

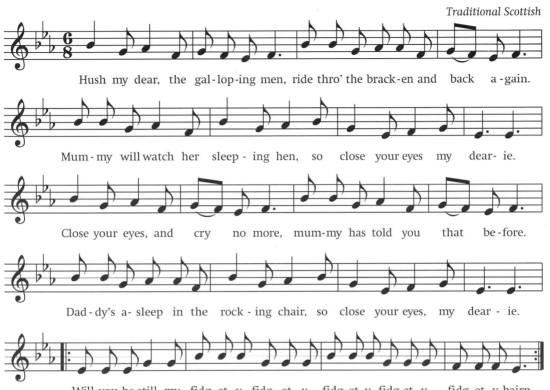

Hush my dear, the gal-lop-ing men, ride thro' the brack-en and back a-gain.

Mum-my will watch her sleep-ing hen, so close your eyes my dear-ie.

Close your eyes, and cry no more, mum-my has told you that be-fore.

Dad-dy's a-sleep in the rock-ing chair, so close your eyes, my dear-ie.

Will you be still, my fidg-et-y, fidg-et-y, fidg-et-y, fidg-et-y, fidg-et-y bairn.

Ahrirang

Korean folk song

Turn ye to me

Traditional Hebridean from Scotland

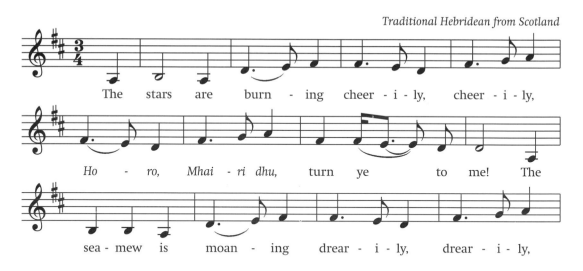

The stars are burn - ing cheer - i - ly, cheer - i - ly,

Ho - ro, Mhai - ri dhu, turn ye to me! The

sea - mew is moan - ing drear - i - ly, drear - i - ly,

Ho - ro, Mhai - ri dhu, turn ye to me!

Cold is the storm-wind that ruf - fles his breast. But

warm are the down - y plumes lin - ing his nest;

Cold blows the storm there, soft falls the snow there,

Ho - ro, Mhai - ri dhu, turn ye to me!

2 The waves are dancing merrily, merrily
Ho-ro Mhairi dhu, turn ye to me!
The sea-birds are wailing wearily, wearily
Ho-ro Mhairi dhu, turn ye to me!
Hushed be thy moaning, lone bird of the sea,
Thy home on the rocks is a shelter to thee
Thy house the angry wave, mine but the lonely grave,
Ho-ro Mhairi dhu, turn ye to me!

Nina, Buschi

Traditional Swiss

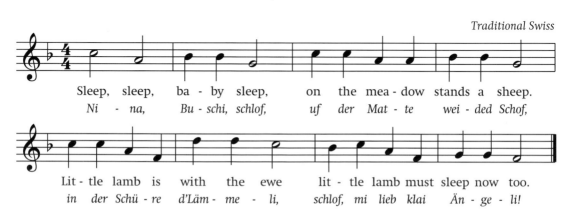

Sleep, sleep, ba - by sleep, on the mea - dow stands a sheep.
Ni - na, Bu - schi, schlof, uf der Mat - te wei - ded Schof,

Lit - tle lamb is with the ewe lit - tle lamb must sleep now too.
in der Schü - re d'Läm - me - li, schlof, mi lieb klai Än - ge - li!

Cradling song

Lisa Weinstein, America

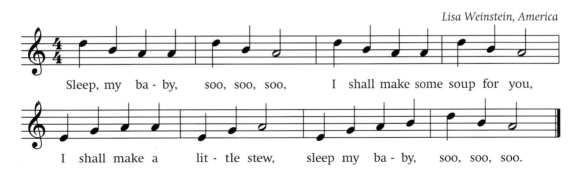

Sleep, my ba - by, soo, soo, soo, I shall make some soup for you,

I shall make a lit - tle stew, sleep my ba - by, soo, soo, soo.

2 Sleep, my baby, soo, soo, soo,
Sun and moon may shine on you,
Glitt'ring stars are shining bright,
Guarding you all through the night.

Now all the flowers are sleeping

Die Blümelein, sie schlafen

Traditional German

Now all the flow'rs are sleep-ing in shim-me-ring sil-ver moon-light. Their
Die Blü- me lein, sie schla-fen schon längst im Mon-den-schein, sie

lit-tle heads are nod-ding as soft-ly stirs the night. And
ni-cken mit den Köpf-chen auf ih-ren Sten-ge-lein. Es

gent-ly do the bran-ches sway as fades a-way the day.
rüt-telt sich der Blü-ten-baum, er säu-selt wie im Traum.

Sleep oh sleep, sleep my lit-tle bon-nie babe, hap-py dreams to-night.
Schla - fe, schla-fe, du, mein Kind-lein schla-fe ein!

2 And all the birds were singing
So happy, clear in the sunshine;
But now the birds are resting,
Their evening chorus is done.
The cricket in the barley-field
His chirping is not stilled.
   Sleep oh sleep ...

3 The Sandman comes a-stealing
And looking in through the window,
His shadow on the ceiling
Is cast by firelight's glow.
The sandman then his sand will shake
And sweet dreams will he make.
   Sleep oh sleep ...

Lambs are sleeping

Traditional English

Lull - a - by, oh, lull - a - by, Flow'rs are clos'd and lambs are sleep-ing,

Stars are up, the moon is peep - ing, Lull - a - by, oh, lull - a - by.

While the birds are si - lence keep-ing, Sleep, my ba - by fall a sleep-ing.

Lull - a - by, oh, lull - a - by, Lull - a - by, oh, lull - a - by.

A la nanita nana

Spanish

Rock - a - by ba - by, go to sleep now, go to sleep now,
A la na - ni - ta na - na, na - ni - ta e - a, na - ni - ta e - a,

Fine

My lit - tle Je - sus go to sleep, God bless you, God bless you.
Mi Je - sús tie - ne sue - ño, ben - di - to se - a, ben - di - to se - a.

Lit - tle spark - ling foun - tain, clear and mu - si - cal,
Fuen - te - ci - lla que cor - res cla - ra y so - no - ra,

Night - in - gale of the woods sing - ing all night long.
Rui - se - ñor de la sel - va, can - tan - do llo - ras;

Hush while the cra - dle's rock - ing, swing - ing high in the wind.
ca - llad mien - tras la cu - na se ba - lan - ce - a

Da Capo al Fine

Rock - a - by lit - tle ba - by, rock - a - by, go to sleep.
A la na - ni - ta na - na, na - ni - ta e - a.

29

All is at rest

K v Winterfeld

H v Fallersleben, Germany

All is now still and all is at rest.
Al - les still in sü - ßer Ruh,
Sleep shall now
drum, mein

fill your eye - lids bless'd. Out - side mur - murs gent - ly the
Kind, so schlaf auch du! Drau - ßen säu - selt nur den

breeze And sings its song a - mong the trees.
Wind, su su su, schlaf ein, mein Kind!

Daylight has passed away

Dutch

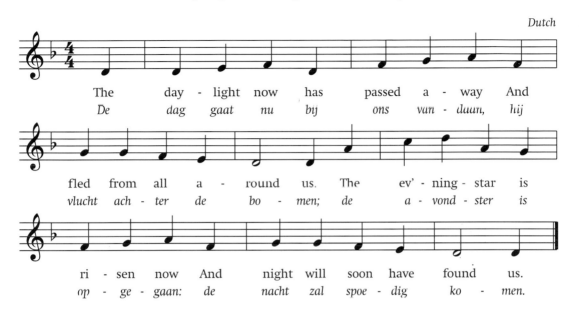

The day - light now has passed a - way And
De dag gaat nu bij ons van - daan, hij

fled from all a - round us. The ev' - ning - star is
vlucht ach - ter de bo - men; de a - vond - ster is

ri - sen now And night will soon have found us.
op - ge - gaan: de nacht zal spoe - dig ko - men.

Hushaby, little one

Traditional Czech

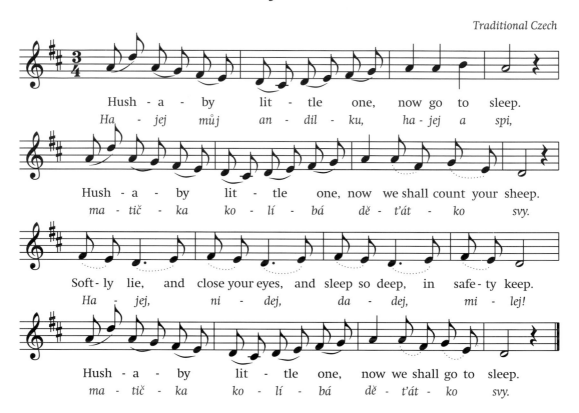

Hush - a - by lit - tle one, now go to sleep.
Ha - jej můj an - dil - ku, ha - jej a spi,

Hush - a - by lit - tle one, now we shall count your sheep.
ma - tič - ka ko - lí - bá dě - ťát - ko svy.

Soft - ly lie, and close your eyes, and sleep so deep, in safe - ty keep.
Ha - jej, ni - dej, da - dej, mi - lej!

Hush - a - by lit - tle one, now we shall go to sleep.
ma - tič - ka ko - lí - bá dě - ťát - ko svy.

Good night to you all

English round

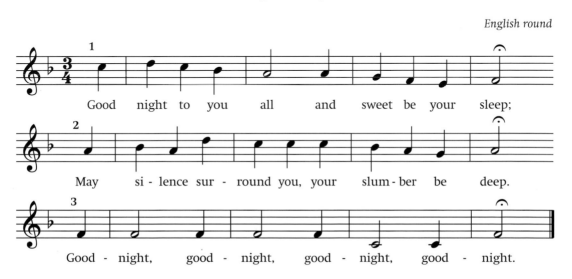

Good night to you all and sweet be your sleep;

May si - lence sur - round you, your slum - ber be deep.

Good - night, good - night, good - night, good - night.

All through the night

Ar hyd y nos

Traditional Welsh

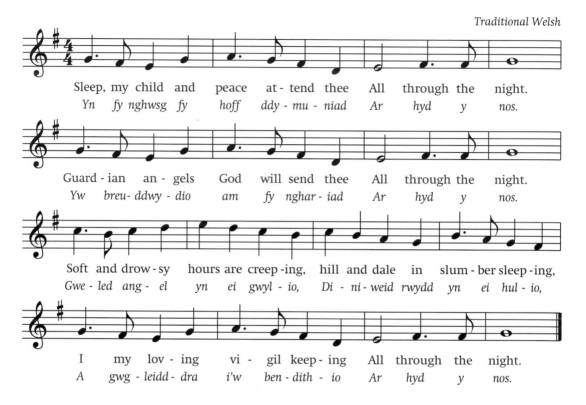

Sleep, my child and peace at-tend thee All through the night.
Yn fy nghwsg fy hoff ddy - mu - niad Ar hyd y nos.

Guard - ian an - gels God will send thee All through the night.
Yw breu - ddwy - dio am fy nghar - iad Ar hyd y nos.

Soft and drow - sy hours are creep - ing, hill and dale in slum - ber sleep - ing,
Gwe - led ang - el yn ei gwyl - io, Di - ni - weid rwydd yn ei hul - io,

I my lov - ing vi - gil keep - ing All through the night.
A gwg - leidd - dra i'w ben - dith - io Ar hyd y nos.

2 Angels watching ever round thee,
    All through the night;
In thy slumbers close surround thee.
    All through the night.
They should of all fears disarm thee.
No forebodings should alarm thee,
They will let no peril harm thee,
    All through the night.

Twinkle, twinkle, little star

Additional verses by Jane Taylor   *Traditional English*

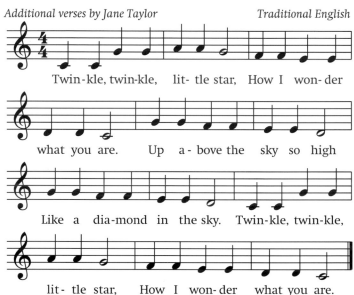

Twin-kle, twin-kle,   lit- tle star, How I   won- der

what you are.   Up   a - bove the   sky so high

Like a   dia-mond in the sky.   Twin-kle, twin-kle,

lit- tle star,   How I   won- der   what you are.

2 When the blazing sun is done
   When he nothing shines upon
   Then you show your little light
   Twinkle, twinkle all the night. Twinkle ...

3 Then the traveller in the dark
   Thanks you for your tiny spark
   He could not see where to go
   If you did not twinkle so. Twinkle ...

4 In the dark blue sky you keep
   Often through my curtains peep
   For that never shut your eye
   Till the sun is in the sky. Twinkle ...

5 As your bright and tiny spark
   Lights the traveller in the dark
   Though I know not what you are
   Twinkle, twinkle, little star. Twinkle ...

'Twixt ox and ass

Entre le boeuf et l'âne

Traditional French

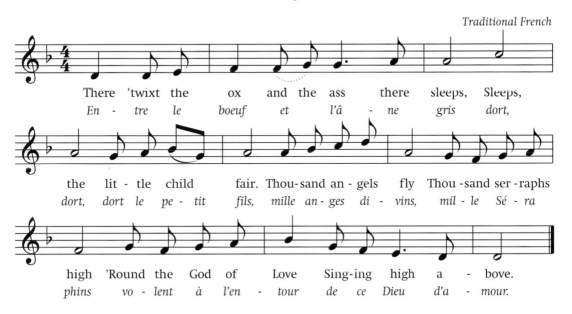

There 'twixt the ox and the ass there sleeps, Sleeps,
En - tre le boeuf et l'â - ne gris dort,

the lit - tle child fair. Thou-sand an - gels fly Thou-sand ser - raphs
dort, dort le pe - tit fils, mille an - ges di - vins, mil - le Sé - ra

high 'Round the God of Love Sing-ing high a - bove.
phins vo - lent à l'en - tour de ce Dieu d'a - mour.

2 There in her arms rocked by Mary there
Sleeps the little child fair.
Thousand angels fly ...

3 Roses are there and the lily there
Sleeps the little child fair.
Thousand angels fly ...

Bye, Baby Bunting

Traditional English

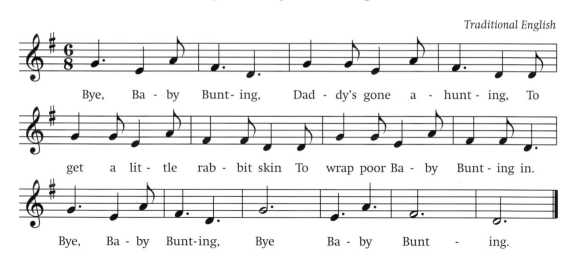

Bye, Ba - by Bunt - ing, Dad - dy's gone a - hunt - ing, To

get a lit - tle rab - bit skin To wrap poor Ba - by Bunt - ing in.

Bye, Ba - by Bunt - ing, Bye Ba - by Bunt - ing.

All the pretty little horses

Traditional Afro-American

Hush - a - by, don't you cry, go to sleep- y lit - tle ba - by.

When you wake, you shall have all the pret - ty lit - tle hors - es.

Blacks and bays, dap - ples and greys, coach and six a - lit - tle hors - es.

Fais dodo

Traditional French

Go to sleep now, my lit-tle ba-by, Go to sleep now, my lit-tle
Fais do-do, Co-las mon p'tit frè-re, fais do-do, t'au-ras du lo-

one. Go to sleep now, my lit-tle ba-by, Go to
lo. Fais do-do, Co-las mon p'tit frè-re, Fais do-

sleep now, my lit-tle one. Your mo-ther rocks you, your mo-ther is
do, t'au-ras du lo-lo. Ma-man est en haut qui fait du gâ-

here. Your fa-ther sees you, your fa-ther is near. Go to
teau. Pa-pa est en bas qui fait du nou-gat. Fais do-

sleep now, my lit-tle ba-by, Go to sleep now, my lit-tle one.
do, Co-las mon p'tit frè-re, fais do-do, t'au-ras du lo-lo.

Nighty-night, my sweet love

Dobrú noc, má milá

Traditional Slovakian

Nigh-ty night, Nigh-ty night, my sweet love. May help be gi-ven by God a-bove

Do - brú noc, má mi-lá, do - brú noc. Nech ti je sám Pán-boh na po-moc!

Nigh-ty night. Sleep deep-ly. I dream that you'll dream sweet-ly.

Do - brú noc, do - bre spi, nech sa ti sní - va - jú slad - ké sny.

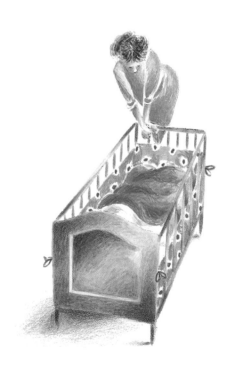

41

Nina bobo

Traditional Indonesian

Ni - na bo - bo, o - ho ni - na - na bo - bo.
Ni - na bo - bo, o ni - na bo - bo.

I shall rock my lit - tle ba - by ni - na bo - bo.
Ka - lau ti - dak bo - bo di gi - git nya - muk.

I shall sing a song o - ho ho o - ho ho.
Ti - dur - lah sa - yang a - dik - ku ma - nis.

I shall rock my lit - tle ba - by ni - na bo - bo.
Ka - lau ti - dak bo - bo di gi - git nya - muk.

All the world is sleeping

Traditional Welsh

Go to sleep up - on my breast, All the world is

sleep - ing. Till the morn-ing's light you'll rest, Mo - ther watch is

keep - ing. Birds and beasts have closed their eyes,

All the world is sleep - ing. In the morn the

sun will rise, Mo - ther watch is keep - ing.

Now let us sing the evening song

From the Odenwald, Germany

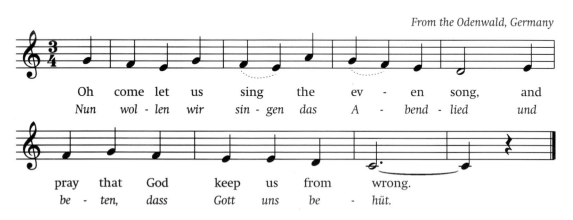

Oh come let us sing the ev - en song, and
Nun wol - len wir sin - gen das A - bend - lied und

pray that God keep us from wrong.
be - ten, dass Gott uns be - hüt.

2 The stars that are shining in heaven tonight
Give blessing with radiant light.

Guten Abend, gut' Nacht

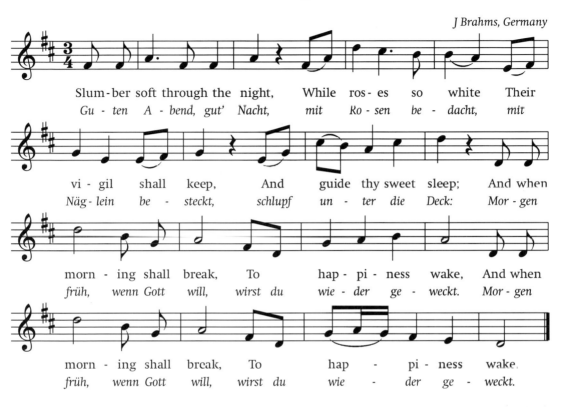

J Brahms, Germany

Slum - ber soft through the night, While ros - es so white Their
Gu - ten A - bend, gut' Nacht, mit Ro - sen be - dacht, mit

vi - gil shall keep, And guide thy sweet sleep; And when
Näg - lein be - steckt, schlupf un - ter die Deck: Mor - gen

morn - ing shall break, To hap - pi - ness wake, And when
früh, wenn Gott will, wirst du wie - der ge - weckt. Mor - gen

morn - ing shall break, To hap - pi - ness wake.
früh, wenn Gott will, wirst du wie - der ge - weckt.

45

Shlof mayn kind

Yiddish

Sleep my child, my beau - ti - ful babe, Sleep my lit - tle son.
Shlof mayn kind, mayn treyst, mayn shey ner, shlof - zhe zu - ne - nyu.

Sleep my child, my pre - cious ba - by, Sleep now, lit - tle one.
Shlof mayn kind, mayn ka - dish ey - ner, shlof - zhe lyu - lyu - lyu.

At your cra - dle sits your mo - ther, Sings a song and cries.
Bay dayn vi - gl zitst dayn ma - me, zingt a lid un veynt.

One far day you may un - der - stand The tears in her eyes.
Vest a - mol far - shteyn mis - ta - me, vos zi hot ge - meynt.

Yankele

Yiddish

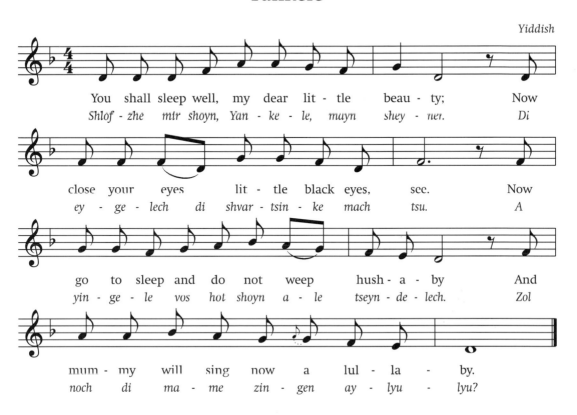

You shall sleep well, my dear lit - tle beau - ty; Now
Shlof - zhe mir shoyn, Yan - ke - le, mayn shey - ner. Di

close your eyes lit - tle black eyes, see. Now
ey - ge - lech di shvar - tsin - ke mach tsu. A

go to sleep and do not weep hush - a - by And
yin - ge - le vos hot shoyn a - le tseyn - de - lech. Zol

mum - my will sing now a lul - la - by.
noch di ma - me zin - gen ay - lyu - lyu?

47

Little cat

Traditional Ukrainian

Puss - y cat, lit - tle grey one, puss - y cat, lit - tle white one
Ko - ti - ku si - ren - ky, ko - ti - ku bi - len - ky,

Hush my puss - y cat now, don't make such a mia - ow.
Kot - ku vo - lo - kha - ty, ne kho - di po kha - ti.

Puss - y cat lit - tle grey one, puss - y cat lit - tle white one,
Ne kho - di po kha - ti, ne bu - di di - tya - ti.

Ba - by's gone to sleep now, you must be so quiet now.
Di - tya bu - di spa - ti, ko - tik vor - ko - ta - ti.

Puss - y cat love - ly lit - tle grey one, Puss - y cat love - ly lit - tle white one,
Oi, na ko - ta vor - ko - ta, na di - ti - nu dri - mo - ta.

A-ha, a-ha, la li la
Ah, Ah, lyu - li!

Sleep, my darling little son

Traditional Ukrainian

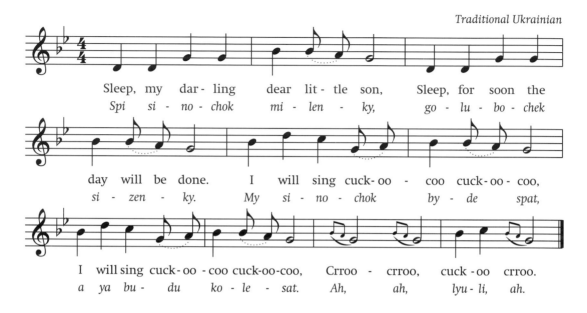

Sleep, my dar - ling dear lit - tle son, Sleep, for soon the
Spi si - no - chok mi - len - ky, go - lu - bo - chek

day will be done. I will sing cuck- oo - coo cuck- oo - coo,
si - zen - ky. My si - no - chok by - de spat,

I will sing cuck- oo - coo cuck- oo-coo, Crroo - crroo, cuck - oo crroo.
a ya bu - du ko - le - sat. Ah, ah, lyu - li, ah.

2 Stormy wind, you blow so wild.
  Must you wake now my little child?
  I will sing such a soft lullaby,
  It shall croon with the wind's whooping cry.
     Crroo-crroo, cuckoo-crroo.

3 Now the wind sighs soft, do you hear?
  Mother's singing; you shall not fear.
  Sings to you such a soft lullaby,
  She will croon with the wind's gentle sigh.
     Crroo-crroo, cuckoo-crroo.

A fairy's love song

Cnochd a bheannichd

Traditional Scottish Highland

Wea-ry me all a lone Gath'-ring brack-en, gath'-ring brack-en;
Tha mi sgìth s'mi leam fhìn Buain a rain-ch, buain a rain-ich;

Wea-ry me all a-lone Gath'-ring brack-en al-ways.
Tha mi sgìth s'mi leam fhìn Buain a rain-ich daonn-an.

Up the hill-side, down the hill-side, Up the hill-side bon-ny
Cul an tom-ain, bràigh an tom-ain, Cul an tom-ain bhoidh each

Up the hill-side, down the hill-side, All day long so lone-ly.
Cul an tom-ain braigh an tom-ain Huil-e lath'-nam m'aon-ar.

Should I see you ap-pear Co-ming o-ver down the hill-side

No more sad would I be With my love be-side me.

Oh, how lovely is the evening

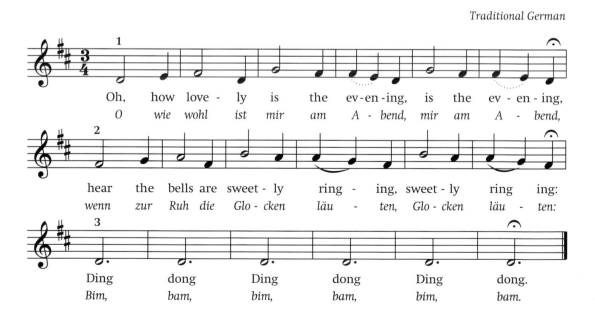

Oh, how love - ly is the ev - en - ing, is the ev - en - ing,
O wie wohl ist mir am A - bend, mir am A - bend,

hear the bells are sweet - ly ring - ing, sweet - ly ring ing:
wenn zur Ruh die Glo - cken läu - ten, Glo - cken läu - ten:

Ding dong Ding dong Ding dong.
Bim, bam, bim, bam, bim, bam.

Maro marotxu

Traditional Basque

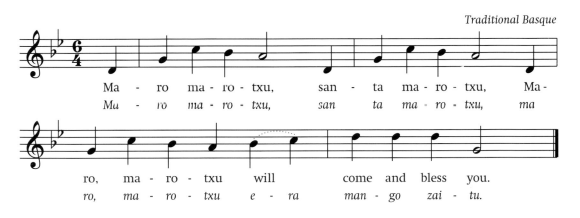

Ma - ro ma - ro - txu, san - ta ma - ro - txu, Ma - ro, ma - ro - txu will come and bless you.

Mu - ro ma - ro - txu, san - ta ma - ro - txu, ma - ro, ma - ro - txu e - ra man - go zai - tu.

Dodo, ma câline

Traditional French

Do - do go to sleep my las - sie Do - do go to
Do - do ma câ - li - ne, do - do

sleep my girl. Do - do go to sleep my lad - die
mon câ - lin. En - dors toi ma câ - li - ne,

Fine

Do - do go to sleep my boy
en - dors toi mon câ - lin.

Ly - ing on my breast, you shall go to rest.
Câ - lin, ma câ - li - ne, dors jus - q'au ma - tin

Da Capo al Fine

Ly - ing in my arms, you shall fear no harm.
au pli de mon bras, au creux de mon sein.

O Lord, abide with us

Herr, bleibe bei uns

Albert Thate, Germany

O Lord, a - bide with us   For   ev - en - tide o'er -
Herr,   blei - be   bei   uns,   denn   es   will   A - bend

takes   us   And the   day - light   swift - ly   fades   a - way.
wer   -   den,   und der   Tag   hat   sich   ge -   nei -   get.

Bayushki bayoo

Russian

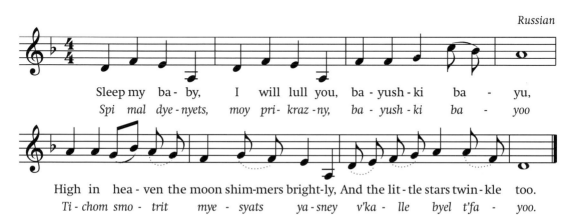

Sleep my ba - by,   I   will lull you, ba - yush - ki   ba - yu,
Spi   mal   dye - nyets,   moy   pri- kraz - ny,   ba - yush - ki   ba   -   yoo

High in   hea - ven the moon shim-mers bright-ly, And the lit - tle stars twin-kle   too.
Ti - chom smo - trit   mye - syats   ya - sney   v'ka - lle   byel t'fa -   yoo.

2 Through the gorges and the country
   Rivers quietly stream.
   Father's riding in the bright moonlight,
   Coming home to you.

Ding, dong, there's the bell

Kling, klang, klockan slår

Swedish shepherds' song

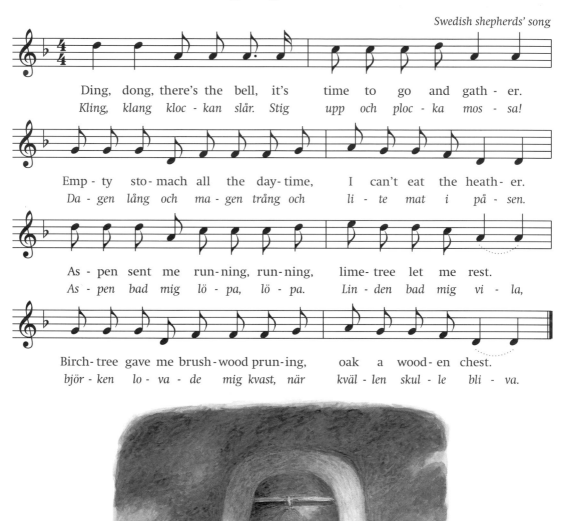

Ding, dong, there's the bell, it's time to go and gath- er.
Kling, klang kloc - kan slår. Stig upp och ploc - ka mos - sa!

Emp - ty sto - mach all the day- time, I can't eat the heath- er.
Da - gen lång och ma - gen trång och li - te mat i på - sen.

As - pen sent me run-ning, run-ning, lime- tree let me rest.
As - pen bad mig lö - pa, lö - pa. Lin - den bad mig vi - la,

Birch- tree gave me brush-wood prun-ing, oak a wood- en chest.
björ - ken lo - va - de mig kvast, när kväl - len skul - le bli - va.

Komoriuta

Translated by Tamako Nina

Traditional Japanese

Sleep, go to sleep my ba-by. Close your lit-tle eyes.
Nen- ne - n yo; o - ko - ro - ri - yo!

My boy is a good ba-by, sleep ba-by sleep.
Bo - ya - wa yoi ko-do nen - ne shi - na.

2 What will be / brought to baby / from yonder town?
   A lovely / flute, and a / deep-sounding drum.

Neyano omiyage nani morata
Denden taikoni she ne fue.

Schlaf, Kindlein, schlaf

Traditional German

Sleep, ba - by, sleep, your fa - ther herds the
Schlaf, Kind - lein, schlaf, dein Va - ter hüt' die

sheep. Your mo - ther shakes the lit - tle tree, and
Schaf, die Mut - ter schüt - telt's Bäu - me - lein, da

down there falls a lit - tle pea, Sleep, ba - by, sleep.
fällt her - ab ein Träu - me - lein. Schlaf, Kind - lein schlaf.

2 Sleep, baby, sleep, in heaven walk the sheep.
 The little stars are little lambs
 The moonbeams are their mother dams
  Sleep, baby, sleep.

3 Sleep, baby, sleep, and you will get a sheep
 And round its neck a golden bell
 The bell will suit him very well.
  Sleep, baby, sleep.

Hush, the waves

Traditional Irish

Hush, the waves are roll - ing in,

White with foam, White with foam.

Fa - ther toils a - mid the din, But

ba - by sleeps at home, at home.

2 Hush the winds roar hoarse and deep,
   On they come, on they come.
   Brother seeks the lazy sheep,
      But baby sleeps at home, at home.

3 Hush the rain sweeps o'er the knowes,
   Where they roam, where they roam.
   Sister goes to seek the cows,
      But baby sleeps at home, at home.

The sandmen

H Diestel, Germany

We are com-ing from the land of moon With a sack of sand and a
Wir kom-men aus dem Mon-den-land, mit ei-nem Sack voll

sil-ver spoon. We stand be-side the bed at night and sprin-kle sand up-
Sil-ber-sand. Wir stehn am Bett-lein in der Nacht, dann wird das Säck-lein

on your sight. Now shut your eyes and go to sleep
auf-ge-macht. Mach dei-ne Au-gen ruh-ig zu,

We sand-men will give one last peep be-fore we go,
und schlumm-re gut, du Kind-lein du! su, su, su, su,

o ho ho. Now go to sleep, go to sleep, go to sleep.
su, su, su; su, su, su, su, su, su, su, su, su, su.

The beech tree

M Garff, Germany

Oh,   how is   the   beech-tree a - rock-ing so   mild? Mm ——— ,
Was schwingt sich die Bu - che so   woh - lig im   Wind? Mm ——— ,

mm ———— .   It   crad-les the   slum-ber - ing bull-finch's   child.
mm ———— .   Sie schau-kelt das schlum-mern-de Buch-fin-ken - kind;

mm ————— ,   mm ————— . The   lit-tlest, the   dear-est, high
mm ————— ,   mm ————— , das   letz - te, das   lieb - ste, hoch

up in the   tree, It   twit-ters, it's dream-ing of   you and of   me.
o - ben im Baum, da   zwit-schert es lei - se, ganz lei - se im Traum.

Mm ——— ,   mm ——— ,   mm ————————— .
Mm ——— ,   mm ——— ,   mm ———————— .

The bamboo flute

Traditional Chinese

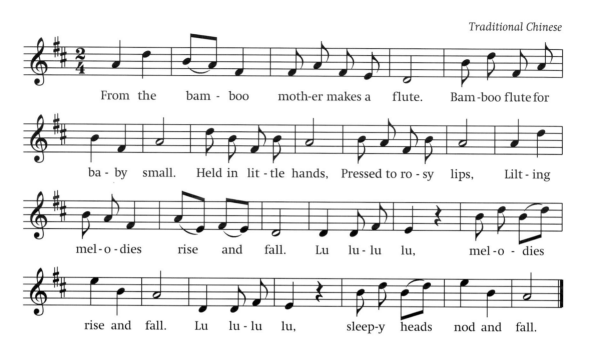

From the bam - boo moth-er makes a flute. Bam-boo flute for

ba - by small. Held in lit -tle hands, Pressed to ro - sy lips, Lilt - ing

mel - o -dies rise and fall. Lu lu - lu lu, mel -o - dies

rise and fall. Lu lu - lu lu, sleep-y heads nod and fall.

Night is here

Cherokee

Night is here, ay ah ah. Stars ap - pear,

ay ah ah, Ma - ma - ma, ay - ah ah ah.

2 Owls you hear, ay ah ah,
   Do not fear, ay ah ah,
     Ma-ma-ma, ay ah ah ah.

3 Close your eyes, ay ah ah.
   Go to sleep, ay ah ah,
     Ma-ma-ma, ay ah ah ah.

Doi doi

Surinam

Doi, doi, pin - pin, ba - by go to slum - ber.

Doi, doi, I will give you a cu - cum - ber.

Oh deary, how weary

Finnish

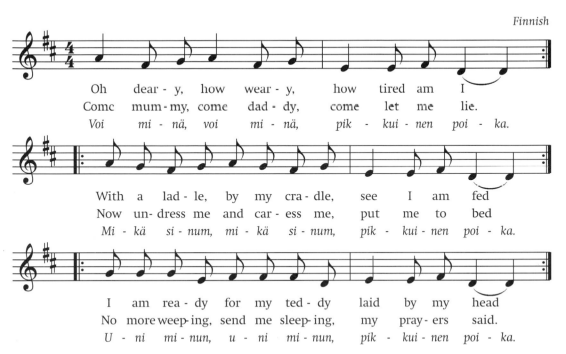

Oh dear - y, how wear - y, how tired am I
Come mum - my, come dad - dy, come let me lie.
Voi mi - nä, voi mi - nä, pik - kui - nen poi - ka.

With a lad - le, by my cra - dle, see I am fed
Now un - dress me and car - ess me, put me to bed
Mi - kä si - num, mi - kä si - num, pik - kui - nen poi - ka.

I am rea - dy for my ted - dy laid by my head
No more weep-ing, send me sleep-ing, my pray - ers said.
U - ni mi - nun, u - ni mi - nun, pik - kui - nen poi - ka.

Sleep my baby, little darling

Traditional Colombian

Sleep my ba - by, lit - tle dar - ling, For the night is draw-ing nigh,
Duer - me ni - ño, pe - que- ñi - to, Que la no - che vie - ne ya,

Please sleep quick - ly, for the sand - man Brings my ba - by
Duer - me pron - to mo - co - ci - to, Que el vien - to - te

lul - la - by. Mm mm mm mm Mm mm mm mm mm mm.
arul - la - rá.

Dormi, dormi, bel Bambin

Traditional Italian

Sleep, oh sleep my bon - ny babe, King Di-
Dor - mi, dor - mi, bel Bam - bin, Re di -

vine. Sleep, oh sleep my bon - ny babe
vin! Dor - mi, dor - mi, fan - to - lin.

Fa la nan- na, dear- est dar - ling. Hea-ven's
Fa la nan- na, o ca - ro fi - glio, Re del

King. Beau - ty bless thy gol - den sleep - ing.
ciel, tan - to bel, gra - zio - so gi - glio.

2 Close your eyes, O Treasure mine, my sweet love.
Close your eyes, O Treasure mine.
Fala nanna, King from above.
My heart's King
   Beauty bless thy golden sleeping.

3 Little babe why do you cry? King Divine.
Comes the frost to hurt your eye?
Fala nanna, O Son of mine.
Paradise.
   Beauty bless thy golden sleeping

Mocking bird

Traditional United States

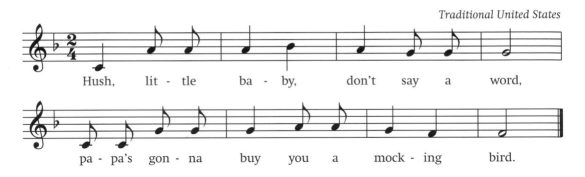

Hush, lit - tle ba - by, don't say a word,

pa - pa's gon - na buy you a mock - ing bird.

2 If that mocking bird don't sing,
   Papa's gonna buy you a diamond ring.

3 If that diamond ring turns brass,
   Papa's gonna buy you a looking glass.

4 If that looking glass gets broke,
   Papa's gonna buy you a billy goat.

5 If that billy goat won't pull,
   Papa's gonna buy you a cart and bull.

6 If that cart and bull turns over
   Papa's gonna buy you a dog called Rover.

7 If that dog named Rover won't bark,
   Papa's gonna buy you a horse and cart.

8 If that horse and cart fall down,
   You'll still be the sweetest baby in town.

Zulu lullaby

Zulu, South Africa

Sleep, lit-tle ba-by, go to sleep, lit-tle ba-by, go to sleep. Your
Sleep, lit-tle ba-by, go to sleep, lit-tle ba-by, go to sleep. Your

fa-ther's on the train, It will take him to the town, And
fa-ther's gone to work, For a year he'll be a-way, And

we must wait.
we must wait. Sad-ly this morn-ing he left you,

Some-where to-night he will think of you. Sleep, lit-tle

ba-by, go to sleep, lit-tle ba-by, go to sleep. The stars are in the

sky, The hills are ly-ing still, And

we must wait.

Sleep, my little baby

Duérmete mi niño

Mexican

Sleep my lit - tle ba - by, sleep-ing now so lone - ly,
Duér - me - te mi ni - ño, Duér - me - te so - li - to,

But when you a - wak - en, Pret - ty toys will greet you.
Que cuan - do te des - pier - tes, Te doy at - ol - i - to.

Golden slumbers

Traditional English

Gol – den slum – bers kiss your eyes, smiles a-
wake you when you rise. Sleep pret-ty dar – ling do not
cry. And I will sing a lul- la – by, lul- la -
by, lul- la – by, lul - la – by.

2 Care you know not, therefore sleep,
   While I o'er you watch do keep.
       Sleep, pretty darling …

Hush ye, my bairnie

Cagaran gaolach

Translated by Malcolm Macfarlane　　　　　　　　　　　　　　*Traditional Gaelic from Scotland*

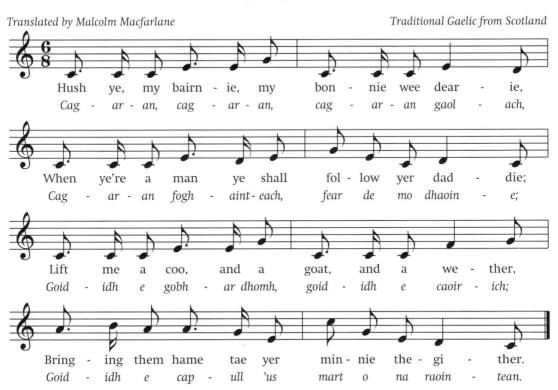

Hush ye, my bairn - ie, my bon - nie wee dear - ie,
Cag - ar - an, cag - ar - an, cag - ar - an gaol - ach,

When ye're a man ye shall fol - low yer dad - die;
Cag - ar - an fogh - aint - each, fear de mo dhaoin - e;

Lift me a coo, and a goat, and a we - ther,
Goid - idh e gobh - ar dhomh, goid - idh e caoir - ich;

Bring - ing them hame tae yer min - nie the - gi - ther.
Goid - idh e cap - ull 'us mart o na raoin - tean.

The Bressay lullaby

Traditional Scottish from Shetland

Ba - loo, ba - lil - li, ba - loo, ba - lil - li, ba -

loo, ba - lil - li, ba - loo - ba. Gae a -

wa', peer - ie fair - ies, Gae a - wa', peer - ie fair - ies, Gae a -

wa', peer - ie fair - ies, Frae oor bairn noo.

Kumbaya

Afro-American

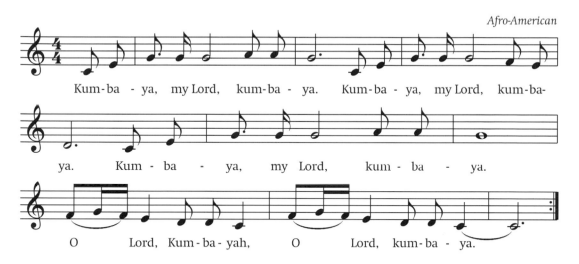

Kum-ba - ya, my Lord, kum-ba - ya. Kum-ba - ya, my Lord, kum-ba-

ya. Kum - ba - ya, my Lord, kum - ba - ya.

O Lord, Kum - ba - yah, O Lord, kum - ba - ya.

2 Someone's sleepin' Lord, kumbaya.

3 Someone's cryin' Lord, kumbaya.

4 Someone's singin' Lord, kumbaya.

5 Kumbaya, my Lord, kumbaya.

Good night, thou beautiful sun

Native American

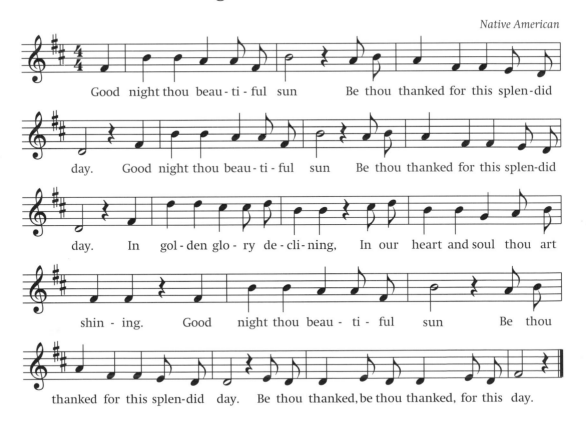

Good night thou beau-ti-ful sun   Be thou thanked for this splen-did

day.   Good night thou beau-ti-ful   sun   Be thou thanked for this splen-did

day.   In   gol-den glo-ry de-cli-ning,   In our   heart and soul thou art

shin-ing.   Good   night thou beau-ti-ful   sun   Be thou

thanked for this splen-did   day.   Be thou thanked, be thou thanked, for this day.

Index

Titles, foreign titles, and *first lines*